W9-BGM-108
3 8542 00028 3157

Capstone   d130114   14.99

PETS' GUIDES

Winnie's Guide to

Caring for Your Horse or Pony

Anita Ganeri

Heinemann
LIBRARY

Chicago, Illinois

Edited by Daniel Nunn, Rebecca Rissman, and Sian Smith
Designed by Cynthia Della-Rovere
Original illustrations © Capstone Global Library Ltd 2013
Illustrated by Rick Peterson
Picture research by Tracy Cummins
Production by Victoria Fitzgerald
Originated by Capstone Global Library Ltd
Printed in China

17 16 15 14 13 12
10 9 8 7 6 5 4 3 2 1

Library of Congress Cataloging-in-Publication Data
Ganeri, Anita, 1961-
  Winnie's guide to caring for your horse or pony / Anita Ganeri.—1st ed.
       p. cm.—(Pets' guides)
Includes bibliographical references and index.
ISBN 978-1-4329-7134-2 (hb)—ISBN 978-1-4329-7141-0 (pb)
1. Horses—Juvenile literature. 2. Ponies—Juvenile literature. I. Title.
SF285.3.G36 2013
636.1'6—dc23   2012017282

Acknowledgments
The author and publisher are grateful to the following for permission to reproduce copyright material: Alamy p. 17 (© Peter Titmuss); Fotolia.com p. 7 (© Sonya Etchison); Getty Images pp. 13 (Margaret Miller), 21 (Simon Clay); iStockphoto pp. 5 (© Francisco Romero), 11 (© Kerstin Waurick), 23 (© Julie Vader), 27 (© Hedda Gjerpen); Shutterstock pp. 9 (© Tamara Didenko), 15 (© Elena Elisseeva), 19 (© Sari Oneal), 25 (© Nagy Melinda).

Cover photograph of a brown horse reproduced with permission of Shutterstock (© Lisa A). Design elements reproduced with permission of Shutterstock (© Picsfive) and Shutterstock (© R-studio).

We would like to thank Margaret Linington-Payne, Director of Standards, British Horse Society, for her invaluable help in the preparation of this book.

Every effort has been made to contact copyright holders of any material reproduced in this book. Any omissions will be rectified in subsequent printings if notice is given to the publisher.

All the Internet addresses (URLs) given in this book were valid at the time of going to press. However, due to the dynamic nature of the Internet, some addresses may have changed, or sites may have changed or ceased to exist since publication. While the author and publisher regret any inconvenience this may cause readers, no responsibility for any such changes can be accepted by either the author or the publisher.

Contents

Do You Want a Horse? 4
Choosing Your Horse. 6
A Healthy Horse 8
Living Outside 10
Living in a Stable 12
Exercise 14
Tack 16
Feeding Time 18
Grooming 20
Hooves and Shoes 22
Calling the Vet 24
On the Move 26
Horse Facts 28
Helpful Tips 29
Glossary *30*
Find Out More *31*
Index *32*

Some words are shown in bold, **like this**. You can find out what they mean by looking in the glossary.

Do You Want a Horse?

Hi! I'm Winnie the horse, and this book is all about horses like me. Keeping horses is great fun, but looking after us takes a lot of time and hard work. It also costs a lot of money. Would you make a good horse owner?

Being a good horse owner means making sure that I'm always cared for. I need a safe place to live, a field to run around in, and food and water. You need to **groom** me and look after me if I'm sick. Then I'll quickly become your best friend.

Choosing Your Horse

Horses like me come in lots of different sizes and colors. I'm a chestnut pony. That means that my coat, **mane**, and tail are golden-brown. A pony is a small horse. Your first horse may be a pony.

A good place to find your pet horse is an animal charity. They take in horses that have been badly treated or are not wanted. They try to find good homes for these horses. They will advise you on the best horse for you.

A Healthy Horse

Choose a horse that has a smooth, shiny coat, bright eyes, and pricked-up ears. My **hooves** are very important. They should not be cracked or split. Always have a horse or pony checked over by an expert before you get it.

Horses like company. In the wild, we live in big groups, called **herds**. If we live on our own, we can feel lonely and unhappy. Make sure that you introduce new horses to each other slowly. It may take them a while to get used to each other.

Living Outside

Horses don't mind living outdoors, but you still need to look after us every day. We must have a shelter where we can get out of the sun and bad weather. We can **graze** on the grass in a field, but make sure that we have clean water to drink.

The field we live in must be big enough for grazing and **galloping** around. Check that the grass is healthy. Some plants can make me sick. If my field gets wet and muddy, make sure that I have a dry place to stand.

Living in a Stable

If you keep a horse like me in a **stable**, you'll need to give me lots of care. Make sure that my stable is big enough, with plenty of fresh air. A stable door is ideal—you can open the top half so that I can look out and see what's going on.

Please check that I have a warm, dry, comfy bed made from straw or wood shavings. Muck out my stable every day. This means taking away any **droppings** and dirty bedding. Then make me a new, clean bed.

Exercise

Horses like me need plenty of exercise to stay healthy. If you keep me outside, I can **gallop** around freely in my field. Make sure that my field has a good, strong fence around it to stop me from escaping!

If I live in a **stable**, please let me out into the field regularly. If I'm stuck inside for too long, I can suffer and become sick. Try to let me out at the same time as some of my friends so that I have company.

Tack

If you want to ride me, you need a **bridle**, **saddle**, and saddle cloth. These are called **tack**. The saddle for you to sit on fits on my back. You need to learn how to put the tack on and how to take it off again after your ride.

If you look after your tack properly, it should last for many years. Wipe it down after every ride, then clean and polish it thoroughly once a week. Look out for any signs of wear and tear.

Feeding Time

Outdoors, I love **grazing** on grass. If I live in a **stable**, I can munch good-quality hay. To keep me healthy, you can also give me special horse feed. Put the feed in a bucket on the ground or in a **manger** attached to the stable wall.

I need to drink lots of water every day, otherwise I can become seriously sick. Please make sure that I always have a supply of clean water in my field and stable.

Grooming

To keep my coat glossy and healthy, please **groom** me regularly. Here's what you need…

Winnie's Gorgeous Grooming Kit

- body brush —soft brush

- stable rubber cloth for polishing coat

- dandy brush —stiff brush

- hoof pick for cleaning **hooves**

- rubber curry comb

- soft sponges for washing face

Winnie's List

Horses that live outside only need a light brush. The oil in their coats helps to keep them warm and dry. Horses that live in **stables** can get dirty and need a full groom every day. It is best to do this after you've been riding.

Hooves and Shoes

If you ride me, my feet carry a lot of weight. You need to look after my feet and **hooves** so that I can walk and run properly. For a start, regularly pick out any mud and stones with a hoof pick.

To stop my hooves from getting too worn down, I need to wear metal horseshoes. A **farrier** makes and fits these shoes. The farrier also trims my hooves—it's like you cutting your nails. I may need new shoes about every four to six weeks.

Calling the Vet

Check me over every day in case I'm sick or have an injury. If I'm not well, my ears will feel cold and I might be sweaty or paw at the ground. Call the vet if you're worried and ask them to come to examine me.

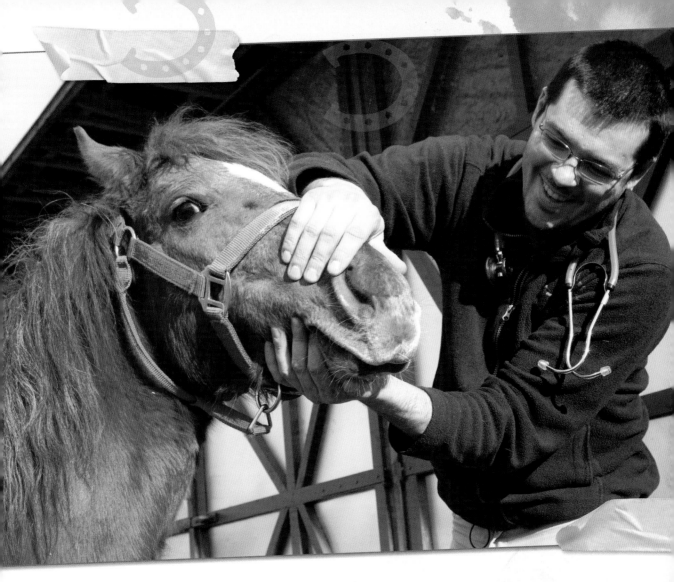

Horses can get nasty stomach aches. They can also have problems with their feet and **hooves**. This can happen if they eat too much rich grass. If this happens, you need to get some medicines from the vet.

On the Move

If you're planning on taking me to shows or competitions, you need a horse **trailer**. You tow this behind your car. Some horses don't like traveling, so practice calmly getting me in and out of the trailer the day before.

Honk if you ❤ Hay!

Make sure that the horse trailer is big enough and has plenty of fresh air. Line it with straw to stop me from slipping, and tie me up inside. Hang up a hay net so that I have something to eat. Don't travel for too long without giving me a break.

Horse Facts

- In the wild, horses spend about 16 to 18 hours of each day **grazing**.

- In some parts of the world, horseshoes are symbols of good luck.

- The height of a horse is measured in "hands." A hand is about 4 inches. A pony is a horse that is less than 14.2 hands high.

- The smallest breed of horse in the world is the Falabella from Argentina. Fully-grown adults stand less than 30 inches high.

Helpful Tips

- Always approach your horse from the side, never from behind. Your horse may be startled if it cannot see you coming.

- Never feed your horse grass clippings or lots of apples. These can make your horse very sick.

- A horse's **hooves** grow all the time so they need trimming regularly. A **farrier** can do this, as well as fitting a horse's shoes.

- If your horse lives outside in winter, it may need a rug to keep it warm. Get a strong, waterproof rug with a warm lining.

Glossary

bridle a leather strap with a noseband and metal ring that fits over a horse's head

droppings horse poo

farrier someone who looks after a horse's feet and fits horseshoes

galloping when a horse is running at its fastest speed

graze eat grass

groom brush and care for your horse's coat

herds large groups of horses

hooves a horse's feet

mane the hair on a horse's head, neck, and back

manger a metal basket attached to a stable wall for a horse's hay

saddle a leather seat put on a horse's back for a rider to sit on

stable a building where a horse is kept when it is not outside

tack the word used for a horse's bridle and saddle

trailer a large box on wheels that is used to carry horses. It is towed behind a car.

Find Out More

Books

Eschbach, Andrea and Markus. *How to Speak Horse*. North Pomfret, Vt.: Trafalgar Square, 2012.

Haas, Jessie. *Horse Crazy!: 1,001 Fun Facts, Craft Projects, Games, Activities, and Know-How for Horse-Loving Kids*. North Adams, Mass.: Storey, 2009.

Monahan, Erin. *Caring for Your Horse*. Mankato, Minn.: Capstone, 2008.

Internet Sites

Facthound offers a safe, fun way to find Internet sites related to this book. All of the sites on Facthound have been researched by our staff.

Here's all you do: Visit www.facthound.com
Type in this code: 9781432971342

Index

animal charities 7

bedding 13

company 9, 15

droppings 13

exercise 14–15

facts and tips 28–29
farrier 23, 29
fields 10–11, 14, 15, 19
food and water 10, 18–19, 29

galloping 11, 14
grazing 10, 11, 18, 28
grooming 20–21

healthy horses 8–9
height of a horse 28
herds 9
hooves 8, 20, 22–23, 25, 29
horseshoes 23, 28
horse trailer 27

illness 11, 15, 19, 24–25

living outdoors 10–11, 14, 21, 29

mucking out 13

ponies 6, 28, 31

saddle 16
shelters 10
stables 12–13, 15, 18, 19, 21

tack 16–17
traveling 26–27

vet 24, 25

wild horses 9, 28